How Shakespeare Saved My Life

A theatrical retelling based on my true stories

Jacob Ming-Trent

methuen | drama

LONDON • NEW YORK • OXFORD • NEW DELHI • SYDNEY

METHUEN DRAMA
Bloomsbury Publishing Plc, 50 Bedford Square, London, WC1B 3DP, UK
Bloomsbury Publishing Inc, 1359 Broadway, New York, NY 10018, USA
Bloomsbury Publishing Ireland, 29 Earlsfort Terrace, Dublin 2, D02 AY28, Ireland

BLOOMSBURY, METHUEN DRAMA and the Methuen Drama logo are trademarks of Bloomsbury Publishing Plc

First published in Great Britain 2026

Cover design and image by Julian Rozzell

A catalog record for this book is available from the British Library.

Library of Congress Control Number: 2026941613

ISBN: PB: 978-1-3505-9594-1
ePDF: 978-1-3505-9595-8
eBook: 978-1-3505-9596-5

Series: Modern Plays

Typeset by Westchester Publishing Services

For product safety related questions contact productsafety@bloomsbury.com.

To find out more about our authors and books visit www.bloomsbury.com and sign up for our newsletters.

How Shakespeare Saved My Life

A theatrical retelling based on my true stories

Jacob Ming-Trent

The world premiere of *How Shakespeare Saved My Life* was produced by Berkeley Repertory Theatre, Berkeley, CA, Johanna Pfaelzer, Artistic Director / Tom Parrish, Managing Director; by Folger Theatre, Karen Ann Daniels, Artistic Director; and by Red Bull Theater, Jesse Berger, Artistic Director, at The Public Theater.

Originally commissioned and produced by Folger Theatre, Karen Ann Daniels, Artistic Director, and by Red Bull Theater, Jesse Berger, Artistic Director.

It ran at Berkeley Repertory Theatre January–March 2026 with the following cast and creative team:

Playwright and Performer	**Jacob Ming-Trent**
Director	**Tony Taccone**
Choreographer	**Tiffany Rachelle Stewart**
Scenic Design	**Takeshi Kata**
Costume Design	**Danielle Preston**
Lighting Design	**Alan C. Edwards**
Sound Design and Original Music	**Jake Rodriguez**
Projections Design	**Alexander V. Nichols**
Stage Manager	**Sofie Miller**
Assistant Stage Manager	**Paige Weissenburger**

It then ran at the Folger Theatre, directed by Tony Taccone, in June 2026.

How Shakespeare Saved My Life

A theatrical retelling based on my true stories

MUSIC!

A man walks to the stage and stops in front of the church pew to say a brief prayer.

Jacob Narrator What's up, my people? Welcome to my ancestors and spiritual protectors. Welcome to all of you. No matter where you come from, what you do or don't do, whom you love or don't love, I love you. Because you've chosen to congregate here today, so thank you for coming, Congregation! My name's Jacob. What are your names? Greetings. Now turn to the person next to you and tell them, "Greetings, thank you for coming." The title of tonight's show is *How Shakespeare Saved My Life*. First, here's what you're not going to see.

Jacob *running. Gunshots.* **Jacob** *goes all* Matrix, *blocking police bullets with his* Complete Works of Shakespeare. *Bullets bounce off the book. Lights up.*

Congregation, that's not how Shakespeare saved my life! This show is a testimony. Stay on your toes, 'cause the road to Shakespearean-sized forgiveness is an odyssey. Today you will see a one-man show. I don't want to be up here all alone, but the American theater don't got no money, so I've got to play all the roles. We had a great band, but we had to cut 'em 'cause of budget cuts. We asked for a DJ, but the National Endowment for the Arts said, "No way," so our stage manager is gonna drop the beat. GO 'HEAD, STAGE MANAGEMENT—DROP THE BEAT! But thank you to the theater for these amazing panels and this beautiful church pew!

The beat drops.

Today, Congregation, I NEED your participation. Every time I point at you, I need you to say, "Play on!" Let's practice . . .

Jacob *points to the* **Congregation**.

Congregation Play on!

Jacob Narrator You got it! Let's begin! Only we won't begin at the beginning, 'cause that's . . . boring. Let's start in 1992. What was going on in 1992? In '92, America elected its first Black president.

Projected images of Bill Clinton playing the saxophone.

Tupac released his first album: *2Pacalypse Now*!

Ghostly images of Tupac.

LA erupted in 1992.

Ghostly images of LA Riots.

An artist named Biggie released his first single: "Party and Bullshit!"

Ghostly images of Biggie.

In 1992, I'm twelve. Me and my family live in Pittsburgh, PA, in a lower middle-class neighborhood in a Rust Belt town. Now you know where we are and when we are, so let's start the play. It starts at . . .

Jacob *jams a bit. Then he cuts the beat.*

. . . six o'clock in the morning. I wasn't yet up and yawning. My father creeped in my room to give me the news.

Pensive music with a sparse sound plays.

Dad Fat man, fat man, wake up. Your mother called the police. I gotta leave the house now. I messed up, fat man. I'll be back, but I don't know when. Remember what I taught you: best thing for a man to be is a good listener. Listen to a man's words. Learn to use ya words. A word can save ya life. I'll be back, fat man. I'll be back.

Jacob Narrator Congregation, I figured he'd be back soon. I got dressed for school. My mother stopped me before I left my room.

Mom I threw your father out. You're the man of the house now. So, grow up. I'm working two jobs. I can't afford to raise you or baby you. When you walk out that door, you're on your own. And this world was not made for you. To them you're a predator, a robber, an assaulter. Jacob, you have to live as though you are permanently in danger. Don't be late for school.

Jacob Narrator Congregation, that was a heavy morning. I put my headphones on and listened to some Pharcyde.

Beat drop. Pharcyde music plays.

And I ran to school. And that's the day I met the word wizard . . .

Musical flourish.

The Stratford scribe . . .

Musical flourish.

The royal rhymer himself . . .

Musical flourish.

William Shakespeare. (*Pharcyde music continues.*) I'm walking down the school hallway with a box of Nerds in my left hand and a bag of Skittles in my right. I open the classroom door with my belly. I walked into the wrong classroom. I didn't know what these fools were tryin' to learn, but it was better than sittin' in math class. So, I dumped the bag of Skittles in my mouth and began listening.

Music out. **Old Teach** *blows his whistle.*

Old Teach Welcome to Shakespeare class!!! Clap it up! Clap it up! Clap it up!

Old Teach *blows the whistle.*

Now shut up!

Jacob Narrator Congregation, our Shakespeare teacher was also our football coach.

Old Teach Billy, you're up! Let's kick some Shakespeare butt. Get in there and make a play.

Billy I'm Billy. This is from *Coriolanus*.

You common cry of curs, whose breath I hate
As reek o' the rotten fens, whose loves I prize
As the dead carcasses of unburied men
That do corrupt my air. You banish me?
Nawwwww, I banish you!
Thus I turn my back. There is a woooooorld elsewhere.

Jacob Narrator When Billy said that, I said, "oh shit!" I imagined speaking to the principal after he suspended me from school.

Principal Mr. Jacob, you are suspended from school!

Jacob Twelve You suspend me? Nawwwww, I suspend you! There is a schoooool for me elsewhere!

Old Teach Jacob, get up off the bench. Join the class. Read this.

Jacob Twelve NAW! Teach, I got extracurriculars coming out my ass! Bye!

Whistle.

Old Teach This is Shakespeare class, no one leaves Shakespeare class without reading a Shakespeare speech. Read it.

Jacob Twelve "We few, we happy few, we band of brothers.
For he to-day that sheds his blood with me
Shall be my brother; be he ne'er so vile,
This day shall gentle his condition."

Yo? What does that mean?

Old Teach It means no matter how low a man's circumstance, if he fights, he will be reborn. Okay, let's make a play! Put your balls in it.

Jacob My balls?

"We few, we happy few, we band of brothers.
For he to-day that sheds his blood with me
Shall be my brother; be he ne'er so vile.
This day shall gentle his condition:
And gentlemen in England now a-bed
Shall think themselves accursed they were not here
And hold their manhood's cheap whiles any speaks
That fought with us upon Saint Crispin's day."

Pause.

How was that?

Old Teach Way to make a play. That was divine.

Jacob Narrator And then . . .

We hear angel music and see a projected image of an angel.

. . . an angel descends into the classroom, touches me on the nose, and tells me, "You will be one of the greatest classical actors of your generation!"

I'm just messin' with you; that shit didn't happen. Congregation, I'll never forget that day. 'Cause when I woke up that morning, I was a super-predator. After that class, I was a Shakespeare prodigy! I was REBORN. Play on!

Congregation Play on!

Jacob Narrator Ninth grade! Me and Shakespeare became partners.

Music.

English Teacher Mr. Jacob, what urban filth are you reading in my English class?

Jacob Fourteen I'm reading *The Merchant of Venice* by William Shakespeare. I'm a Shakespearean actor, so . . . I kinda have to read . . . Shakespeare.

English Teacher (*whispering*) How dare you read Shakespeare in my English class? We are reading *Willy Wonka and the Chocolate Factory*.

Jacob Fourteen Well, *Willy Wonka and the Chocolate Factory* is . . . racist, Ms. Jackson. The Oompa-Loompas are unpaid laborers, smuggled into the country to work for cocoa beans at the "chocolate factory."

English Teacher (*whispering*) How dare you! *Willy Wonka* is an American classic. Get your D-average butt to the principal's office. You are going to detention!

Jacob Fourteen Detention? My mother will kill me. Have mercy, Ms. Jackson. See, brother Shakespeare teaches us sweet mercy is nobility's true badge. The quality of mercy is not strained, Ms. Jackson. It dropeth as the gentle rain from heaven upon the place beneath. It's twice blessed. It blesseth him that gives, and him that takes. Detention? Naw! Open thy gates of mercy, Ms. Jackson. And I promise to read *Willy Wonka and the Chocolate Factory*. Even though its racist.

English Teacher Get your butt back in the room. And no more Shakespeare in my English class!

Jacob Narrator That's right, Congregation! Me and Shakespeare could do anything. Congregation, between me and you, Shakespeare helped me lose my virginity! Wanna see? Play on!

Congregation Play on!

The words "Shakespeare helped me lose my VIRGINITY!" are projected.

Jacob Narrator I'm in Pittsburgh up on August Wilson's Hill at a party. Back then . . .

The stage manager hands **Jacob** *a Pabst Blue Ribbon.*

. . . when I was underage drinking, I drank Pabst Blue Ribbon. As you see on the can . . . it won a blue ribbon! Kids, no underage drinking. I'm at the party scoping it out, and I spot a gorgeous young lady. I ask her name. She said Sylvia. I knew what I had to do.

Jacob *locates a woman in the* **Congregation**.

Hey, how you doing? Enjoying the show? Nice outfit! The theater can't afford another actor, so I need a volunteer. You have no lines. All you have to do is be gorgeous. And you are gorgeous, so this is the perfect role for you. Are you ready? Stage management, drop the beat.

Music plays. The lights change. The room takes on a romantic vibe.

Jacob Sixteen
"What light is light, if Sylvia be not seen?
What joy is joy if Sylvia be not by?
Unless it be to think that she is by
And feed upon the shadow of perfection?
Except I be by Sylvia in the night,
There is no music in the nightingale.
Unless I look on Sylvia in the day,
There is no day for me to look upon.
She is my essence, and I leave to be
If I be not by her fair influence
Fostered, illumined, cherished, kept alive.
I fly not death, to fly his deadly doom.
Tarry I here, I but attend on death,
But fly I hence, I fly away from life."

Jacob Narrator Then, me and Sylvia went into the kitchen pantry and had sweet virginal sex.

(*to the* **Congregation** *member*) Thanks for helping me lose my virginity. I mean, for helping to show how Shakespeare helped me lose my virginity. Please take your seat.

(*to the* **Congregation**) Congregation, after losing my virginity in the kitchen pantry, I walked home in an intense post-coital glow.

"God Bless the Child" plays.

Mother Jacob, it's two in the morning. You have a curfew. I can smell the alcohol from here. You're rebellious. You think the rules don't apply to you. That's going to change today.

Clifford asked me to marry him. I'm engaged. This engagement is a blessing. I get a husband, and you get the father you've been needing!

Jacob I have a father—two fathers—that's too much, son.
Remember what a grace was seated on dad's brow?
Hyperion's curls, the front of Jove himself,
An eye like Mars' to threaten and command,
A station like the herald Mercury
New-lighted on a heaven-kissing hill—
A combination and a form indeed
Where every god did seem to set his seal
To give the world assurance of a man.
Your fiancé? Have you eyes?
You cannot call it love, for at your age
The heyday in the blood is tame, it's humble,
And waits upon the judgment.
And what judgment would leave my dad for your fiancé.
O shame, where is thy blush?

Mother Shame! Shame on you. And don't speak that Shakespeare at me, boy. I knew you would react this way. Selfish! You have your father's selfish gene. You can't be happy for me. After all I've sacrificed for you, you can't support your mother? If you don't recognize Clifford is the father you've been needing, then you cannot be a part of this family. Out! Out of my house! And take that Shakespeare with you! Leave!

The door slams.

Jacob You don't like Shakespeare? I can speak Greek. Maybe, like Icarus, I flew to close to the sun. But a son's love of a father shouldn't deprive a son of a home. Prometheus was banished. The Titans were banished. But they were gods, so they survived. Like Icarus, you can burn my wings and just ground me. As a teen, exile for me means death. Let me stay—I'll be as quiet as a church mouse. Or I'll be a dove and sleep on the roof. You won't even hear this dove cry. I'll be a dust mite so slight you won't feel my presence. Let me stay.

Hello? Hello? That's the end of my speech.

Jacob Narrator Congregation, I called my dad.

The sound of a disconnected phone.

Operator This number has been disconnected.

Jacob Narrator Congregation, I'm sixteen years old. I'm homeless.

The class bell rings.

But I still had to go to school.

Music.

Physics Teacher Hi, kids! Welcome to Junior Physics. This year, we'll be studying black holes. Black holes are so dark and dense that light cannot escape them. In my class, you'll feel as if you've been abandoned in the middle of the ocean and you are about to DIE a horrible drowning death! If you survive, you'll be welcome to the wonderful world of physics. Mr. Jacob, where are you going?

Jacob Sixteen Outta here! Only I'm going nowhere, 'cause I'm homeless. But if you want me to stay, okay! I'll play the villain. Ophelia drowned for love—sad, but true. Would Ophelia drown for physics? No, boo. This noble mind here is overthrown. Teacher, I ain't got time. I got food, water, and shelter on my mind. You want me to learn how to survive your physics class? Someone needs to teach me how to survive life. To learn physics is a privilege for those living a privileged existence. I'm homeless, and it don't feel nice. Is there an equation to figure out what homelessness does to a young life? Did Einstein figure out a formula for what lack of sleep and food does to a growing brain? It could drive you insane, mad. This is madness. Yet there is method in it, if you listen to my logic. Physics? Naw. Teach me how to cheat on my taxes. Teach me how to play the margins so I can stock stocks and win the market. Then, I could afford some brain space to debate whether it's nature or nurture or the Big Bang that brought the universe and me into being. But until my personal circumstances alter or the world creates some change, physics is a luxury. If you want me to learn it, you gotta pray for me . . . or let me borrow some money. Till then, to my own self I must be true. Can't afford physics right now, boo.

Jacob Narrator I quit physics! I dropped out of high school! Congregation, if I didn't make a move, my life would be over soon. I grabbed onto the only lifeline I knew: Shakespeare. Acting is the only profession that doesn't require good grades! But how do you become a Shakespeare actor? I knew who to call.

Gospel music. **Jacob** *picks up an old red phone and dials. Gospel music out.*

God Voiceover You've reached God. The erector of the universe, the original baby daddy. Your favorite show runner. The guardian of the galaxy. What's up, my people!?

Jacob God! It's Jacob. That was a long introduction. I got big problems, God!

God Voiceover Jacob! My chubby brown brother! I'm sitting here at Red Lobster, enjoying these Cheddar Bay Biscuits, taking a brief break from whoopin' the Devil's ass.

Jacob Sixteen With all due respect, God, can we talk about the biscuits later? This is serious shit. My mother kicked me out. I dropped out of high school. But I found this Shakespeare dude. I think he can save my life.

God Voiceover Willy? I know Willy Shakespeare. We play *Mario Kart* together.

Jacob Sixteen God, please stay on topic. How do I become a Shakespeare actor?

God Voiceover Move to New York and sign up for classical training.

Jacob Sixteen Thanks, God! You always got the answers. Enjoy the biscuits.

God Voiceover That's why they call me God! Peace and love!

Jacob *hangs up the phone.*

Jacob Narrator That's how God sounds when he talks to me. I don't know how he sounds when he talks to you. Congregation, I got on the Greyhound bus in Pittsburgh.

The sound of the bus driving off.

Got off in Times Square.

The sounds of New York City.

No high school diploma. No friends. I rented an apartment in Sheepshead Bay, Brooklyn.

A square of light the size of an apartment is projected onto the stage.

Apartment? Closet!

The apartment-sized square of light becomes a rectangle the size of a closet.

And I signed up for "Shakespeare training."

Light change. Music out. Classroom.

Old White Man You are a murderer! A murderer!

Jacob Narrator This is my Shakespeare teacher. Sounds British, but later we found out his ass was from the Bronx. This is what he thought of my acting . . .

Old White Man You're a murderer of the English language! Frankly, my dear boy, you sound . . . Black. Class, if J. B. Smoove and Oprah Winfrey had a baby, Jacob is what the baby would sound like. But your more egregious sin is, you sound . . . fat. Like your vocal chords are greased with fried-chicken drippings or baby back rib sauce. Tragically, you are fat, Mr. Jacob. And I don't mean to make fun of the afflicted, but you cannot play Henry the Fifth. Fat Black people cannot play heroes, Mr. Jacob. Sadly, there are no roles in Shakespeare for you. If you must do Shakespeare, lose weight immediately. And do your best to sound like me! WHITE. Shakespeare was written by a white man for white people. Who's next?

Light change.

Jacob Narrator Congregation, has anyone ever told you you don't sound right or you don't look right? What did you do? I went back to my closet, put on my headphones, and I listened to the heroes.

Back in **Jacob***'s closet. He sits on the church pew and puts on headphones. We hear quotes from Tupac, Malcolm X, Martin Luther King, Jr., Fred Hampton, Biggie, and Muhammad Ali. We see video clips and hear music.* **Jacob** *takes off his headphones, and the music ends. Lights transform the classroom into a rap concert.*

Congregation, I went back to acting class.

Jacob Sixteen Friends, classmates, countrymen, lend me your ears. This teacher's using Shakespeare to whitewash me. He's feeding me his culture and calling it acting technique. You ain't Prospero, bro, and I ain't Caliban. The English language—it's mine, man. You tried to use the Bard to lock me behind bars, but I'm using the Bard's words like Popeye used spinach. I'm growing stronger from the Swan of Avon's lyrics. Everything Shakespeare you fed me, meant to oppress me, I ingested it, turned it into sustenance. Now I'm using the Bard to bend your prison bars, and I'm breaking my feet free. Now I'm a Shakespearean beast tearing down your old school. Guess who you lookin' at—the leader of the new school. And the first lesson imma teach you—imma put your Shakespeare on the ones and twos for you.

Musical hit.

Imma scratch him, remix him.

Musical hit.

Imma roll Shakespeare in some flour and Black seasonings. Imma shake him up, fry him up, put him on a waffle, hot sauce him up, and fucking feed him back to you.

Music comes all the way in.

I'm leveling up right in front of you. Standing like a greyhound upon the start, ready to explode with my rhetorical skills the ivory towers you've built. To fight your institution, some say I'm embracing my destruction. To be or not to be? I choose to be.

Class, that's the end of my lecture.

Music drops.

Teacher, any questions?!

Music restarts. **Jacob** *celebrates and dances. Music out.*

Jacob Narrator Congregation, I didn't say any of that! I said something like that. I beat that teacher! But it didn't feel like a victory. Congregation, why do we have a hard time claiming our victories? I went home.

Projection of the word "HOME." "God Bless the Child" plays.

Mom What are you doing here? Don't tell me. You quit acting school? And now you need your mother to help you figure out why? I don't have much time. So Imma give it to you straight. Your problem is you think you're special! And you're not. I know, because you came from my womb. You have do what everyone else has to do! What everyone else has to do. And you're Black—you can't afford to be frivolous or sensitive. This Shakespeare school? The teacher probably told you you weren't special, so you quit, and now you want to come home. Only this isn't your home, Jacob. You have to stand on the two feet God gave you. You have to accept the truth of who you are. What you are. Or else the world will beat you and beat and beat until you submit to reality or the life is beaten out of you. You're not special, Jacob. I have a tennis lesson.

Jacob Narrator Congregation, I was searching for some kinda home. The word "home" is a synonym of "love." My mother didn't want to give it to me. So, I went looking for my father. He was living—Congregation, you ever hear the expression "the wrong side of town"? My dad was living on the wrong side of the wrong side of town.

Dad *is on the floor searching for something in the rug.*

Dad Fat man! Faaat maan! Welcome home! Thank God you're here. I need ya help, son. I'm looking for my medicine. Can't be but a few places 'cause I sold all the furniture except that church pew. Sold my typewriter. Help me find this medication!

Dad *recovers, realizing he needs to be a father.*

If ya hungry, I got bread an' butter. You can make a butter sandwich! Man, when you was a boy, you loved a butter sandwich. When you was a boy, you'd eat one a day. Wish you had called. There's no phone, but if you told me you was coming, I could a prepared somethin'. You go see your mother? You should see ya mother.

Jacob Sixteen I quit acting school. She, she said I wasn't welcome. I need a place to stay.

Dad She said ya not welcome!? You're not welcome? Your mother's changed. She different. I wish you knew your mother the way I knew her. I was so in love with your mother, just the thought of her would make my feet move. First time ya mother . . .

Lights change to create a romantic feel.

She was floatin' . . .

We hear an uplifting jazz tune.

I was an English major at Boston University, but I was studyin' to be a pickpocket in Roxbury.

I was standin' in front the church as the sun was setting, lookin' for a pocket to pick, just as I saw a pocket that needed picking. Ya mama came floatin' down the steps of the church. She was wearing this long, white, tight-fittin' dress. She looked like the subject of a late Romantic era painting. Only the painting was moving, moving to the rhythm of a Coltrane tune. When ya mama went floatin' by, man, she smelled good. She smelled like fresh, fresh air with a bit a lavender in it.

I was scared to speak to her. She seemed fragile—like if I uttered the wrong syllable she could break. Then I noticed a man following your mother. He was eyeing her and her purse. He was a criminal. I recognized him, 'cause I was a criminal. Just as he was about to make his move on her, I ran up and—

Dad *acts out the fist fight between him and the thief.*

I put my foot to his ass and sent him running down the block. Your mother was startled. I said, "I'm sorry, ma'am, but that hooligan was about rob you." She said, "Oh, thank you." I said, "Ma'am, there's a lot criminals and pickpockets out here. May I have the pleasure of escorting you wherever it is you may be going this beautiful Sunday evening?" She said, "Yes, yes you may." She recognized she was a damsel and I was her Black knight. We talked. I walked. She floated. Then magically, Jacob, I began float too. We floated all the way to your mother's front door. That's when

I laid on her my favorite Shakespeare quote: "Hear my soul speak: the very instant that I saw you did my heart fly at your service and there resides to make me slave to it." Then she kissed me and floated into her apartment. I danced all the way home.

Music swells. **Dad** *dances.*

We married two months later. Then God gifted us a son and we named him Jacob. Remember, Jacob, you were conceived out of a righteous and beautiful Black love. But then your mother changed. She changed.

Dad *finds the medication.*

There it is! My medicine! Now I gotta take it. Stay here. You're seventeen, Jacob. You shouldn't be on the street.

Dad *sits on the pew and wraps a rubber tube around his arm.*

Welcome home, fat man. I missed you.

Jacob Narrator Congregation, I couldn't watch my dad poison himself, so I snuck out of the house. The brightest light in the neighborhood was the chapel of the local church. I figured there I'd find a place to sleep. I entered the chapel and met the minister . . .

Jacob *enters the church.*

Preacher Stay back! You motherfucka, I will not let you rob this church again! If you move from that spot, I'll wear your ass out with this broom stick. Wouldn't be the first stick I stuck up an ass either!

Beat. The **Preacher** *looks* **Jacob** *over.*

You're no robber. If you are in need of spiritual guidance, the church is closed! We open at nine, we close at nine. Monday through Sunday. Three hundred and sixty-five days a year. The God phone is disconnected. We were unable to pay the bill. I've listened to prayers all day. I'm famished. I have a Trader Joe's chicken tikka masala waitin' on me, so the church, goddamit, is closed!

The **Preacher** *pauses as if he's listening to something.*

God is speaking to me. He's avowing to me that you are in danger and that I should offer whatever assistance I can. We are in arears on the light bill, young man. The chapel lights are on a timer. In a few minutes, this chapel will be as dark as Sidney Poitier's ass. Speak . . . speak!

Jacob Seventeen Pastor, I'm no robber. I'm a Shakespearean actor. But I got a question: why is it that everywhere I go, I feel unwanted or in danger? And I need a place to sleep.

The **Preacher** *sits on the church pew.*

Preacher A long time ago, there was a beautiful Black boy, not much younger than you. He was smart, inquisitive; he liked to tell jokes. He enjoyed making people laugh. For summer vacation, his mother sent him to stay with his aunt and uncle in a small town. There, the boy, as he was wont to do, told jokes. A few folks in the town were not amused. So, one evening, men came looking for the boy. They dragged him into the night. There, they cut off his ear, knocked out his teeth, beat his eye out of its socket. Wrapped a seventy-five-pound fan around his neck, shot him. Then they threw the child off a bridge into the river. All this for a ill-timed joke. You see, boys like you have always been unwanted. Boys like you have always been in danger.

Jacob Seventeen Preacher, I need a place to sleep.

The lights shut off. Only the moonlight remains.

Preacher If anything happens to you in this chapel, we will lose our limited liability insurance. Now, little sheep, I must send you out amidst the wolves.

Jacob *walks toward the* **Congregation**.

Jacob Narrator On the steps of the church, I felt alone in a cosmic sense. Like no one in the entire universe cared for me. Congregation, have you ever felt that alone? That's when I heard this . . .

Music.

That music led me to a park, where some DJs were throwing a party. I sat on a bench and listened. Some people don't want me to tell this part of the story, but, Congregation, I got to. Play on!

Congregation Play on!

Popeye Hey, you like jokes? What does Michael Jordan put on his biscuits? Space jam. They call dat a dad joke. They call me Popeye 'cause I got a lotta muscles, and I eat spinach, and I love a two-piece and a biscuit. What's your name? You hungry? Wanna candy bar?

Jacob Seventeen I'm Jacob. Yeah, I'm hungry.

Jacob *takes the candy bar.*

Popeye What are you doin' here, Jacob? You like the music?

Jacob Seventeen Yeah, I like the lyrics. Lyrics tell me someone is feeling how I'm feeling.

Popeye That's cool man. What do you do?

Jacob Seventeen Imma Shakespearean actor.

Popeye OH SHIT! That's weird.

Jacob Seventeen What do you do?

Popeye I work in the park. You sittin' here alone, man. I'm worried for you. You vulnerable. It's not safe. Come hang wit my crew, maybe be a part of us. We could use a dude like you.

Jacob Seventeen Yeah, okay. Where your crew at?

Popeye OK!!!! Let me introduce you. Follow me!

Music comes in for no more than 4 or 8 bars, then out.

YOOOO! Yo! Yo! Yo! Yo! Introduce yourselves to Jacob. He wants to join the crew.

Toilet They be callin' me Toilet, 'cause I love talkin' shit. What's up, maaaan!?

Backwash Eyy yo! They call me Backwash 'cause I repeat everything. Everything, everything . . . like backwash.

Jacob Seventeen Hello, I'm Jacob, like the father of Israel.

Backwash This dude sucks. He sucks. He sucks like that White House intern.

Popeye Shut up! To be in the crew, Jacob, you gotta pass a few tests. Tonight, we playin' the Dozens!! Rap-battle style. We play the Dozens to prove you know how to use ya words. You'll be okay, just use that Shakespeare shit. Let's show 'em how it's done.

Popeye *walks toward the* **Congregation**.

Backwash versus Toilet. The winner fights for the title. Pay attention, 'cause you may have to help me choose the winner. Go 'head, drop the beat!

Beat drops.

Backwash Toilet, I saw your mama the other day. Yo mama's old. Yo mama's so old she used to babysit Jesus. Yo mama's so old she took Moses to the prom. She was there when God said, "Let there be light!" Damn, your mama's old. Is the chick alright!?

Toilet My mama old. She old. Yo mama's fat. Yo mom's so fat she's in a sci-fi thriller, looking like Kong after he ate Godzilla. That tsunami the other day? That was your fat mama going to the beach, man, and putting her big toe in the waves.

Popeye *approaches the* **Congregation**.

Popeye Okay, folks, make some noise if you think Backwash won! Make some noise if you think Toilet won!

The **Congregation** *picks the winner with their cheering.*

The winner is . . . Backwash/Toilet. But can Jacob take the belt? Toilet/Backwash versus Jacob.

Toilet/Backwash This gon' be easy man. Jacob, yo mama's short. Yo mama's so short, she don't got a neck or waist. She just a big head on some tiny legs. I saw her feet in her driver's license picture. Who would let this undersize midget drive? But I figured it out—yo mama drives standing up! That's how the bitch is still alive.

Jacob Seventeen Yo, give me a new beat! My mama's short. But yo mama's stupid. I asked your mom her IQ. She said, "How do you spell that?" I gave her a bag of M&M's and asked her to spell "M&M's." She said, "I can't do that." I saw her staring at a glass of orange juice for like twelve days straight. I said, "Why are you doing that?" She said, "The box said 'concentrate.'"

Popeye This one is easy. The winner is . . . Jacob. Jacob, the Black Shakespeare.

A circle of light appears center stage. **Jacob** *steps in it. We hear the sound of loud cheering.* **Jacob** *lifts his hands in the air as a winner!*

Jacob Seventeen Okay, Popeye, I passed your Dozens test. What test is next? This is fun.

Jacob Narrator Congregation, the crew told me to come back to the park around two in the morning. So I was back in the park at two in the morning.

Music. **Jacob** *is still standing in the circle of light.* **Popeye** *and the crew circle* **Jacob**. *We see them in the shadow of the light.*

Popeye Gather around. It's time for the beatdown! Tonight, Jacob, we gotta test your heart literally and figuratively. How do we do that? We gonna stand in a circle and take turns whoopin' your ass. We call it the beat-in.

Toilet When we done, maaan, ya face gon' look like the Hamburglar had a baby with the Cookie Monster. Sorry, maaan.

Backwash Tell this Teletubby the rules. Can't wait to see his face when he hear da rules. Da rules!

Toilet Rules is . . . THERE AIN'T NO RULES!!! Hahahaha.

Backwash Can we gouge Jacob's eyes? I wanna gouge Black Shakespeare in the eyes. In his eyes!

Popeye NO EYE GOUGING. We like you, Jacob! But the world don't like us. So we gotta make sure you tough.

Toilet Look at him he scared, man. He scared, man.

Jacob Seventeen Scared? Let's go! I'm not scared.

Jacob Narrator Congregation, I was scared. Popeye had more muscles in his upper lip than I have in my whole body. The crew balled up their fists and ran toward me.

The beating commences. Every time **Jacob** *is hit, colorful words like "POW," "KAPOW," "BLAP," and "KRAK" are projected.* **Jacob** *falls. He's been knocked out!*

I woke up on Popeye's porch seven hours later. I was hurt. I was peeing out of my butt and pooping out of my penis for a week! But I loved it! It felt like love to me. Congregation, how far will you go for love? Play on!

Congregation PLAY ON!

Jacob Narrator The crew had rituals, just like church.

Popeye Jacob, we want to welcome you into the crew. We do that by smoking weed. If the streets is the church, weed is like communion. We call it the devil's lettuce, the evil edamame, or my favorite, the smoochie poochie.

Popeye *offers* **Jacob** *the joint.*

Jacob Seventeen I don't get high.

Toilet But weed cleanses our mind, our spirits, our colons.

Backwash What kinda dude loves Shakespeare and hates weed? Next he's gonna try to tell us Burger King is better than McDonald's. Burger King is not better than McDonald's.

Popeye Jacob, Black people been smokin' weed for millions and millions of years. I know. I done the research.

Jacob *takes the joint.*

Jacob Narrator I hesitated to smoke 'cause my dad was a drug addict. But I was in the family now, and the family did drugs, so I did drugs.

Jacob *hits the joint.*

Then we sat on Popeye's porch and talked poetry.

The crew passes the joint during this scene.

Jacob Seventeen Shakespeare! He's the greatest poet of all time. He has better bars than Tupac or Biggie.

Backwash WHAT!? Imma kill myself. No way some four-hundred-year-old dead white dude who wore leggings got better bars than Pac an' Biggie.

Toilet Biggie! The greatest. He talk like us. Get high like us. He smells like us. He dropped out of school like us. He a genius, just like we genius.

Jacob Seventeen Shakespeare didn't finish school. Pac didn't finish school. I didn't finish school.

Backwash Tupac the best! Spit lyrics like KRS-One, spit wisdom like Malcolm. Pac was America's worst nightmare. That's why they shot him in Vegas. His death is a mystery, yo. If they shot Britney Spears in Vegas, they'd shut down the whole entire city.

Jacob Seventeen Listen. To be or not to be, that is the question. Whether 'tis nobler in the mind to suffer the slings and arrows of outrageous fortune or to take arms against a sea of troubles and by opposing them end them. BARS!

Backwash To be or not to be? That rhyme is the worst rhyme in the history of humankind! Shakespeare is ass. He's the deepest darkest stankiest part of the ass!!!

Toilet Popeye, didn't Shakespeare get so high, he set himself on fire? Ain't Shakespeare in rehab?

Popeye That was Richard Pryor, clown. Pryor's alive! Shakespeare's dead. Shakespeare died a few weeks after Jesus. Jesus and Shakespeare was boys. They was like the Tupac and Biggie of Bethlehem.

Jacob Seventeen The people that run the Ivy League worship Shakespeare, and they educate the people that run the country. Being Black and knowin' Shakespeare is good business, bro. People will treat you like a superhero.

Backwash Jacob, you right. If Shakespeare makes dollars, then Shakespeare makes sense.

Jacob *hits the joint.*

Jacob Narrator Right then, I hit the joint again, and suddenly, Congregation, my heart started to race 'cause the joint was laced with . . .

Melodramatic, ominous music.

PCP! Congregation, who knows about PCP? For those who don't know . . .

Light change, music video moment. The PCP song.

PCP, Angel Dust, Animal Trank, Rocket Fuel was invented in an American laboratory by an evil scientist who went to evil science school. In the fifties, the doc would give it to ease ya pain. PCP creates delusions of supreme strength. PCP will make you think you's a super dude. But it isn't true! It's just the Angel Dust, the Rocket Fuel, the Animal Trank talkin' to you. It's the PCP, the PCP, the PCP.

ON PCP!!!

Mario video game images appear. We see the Mario dragon, Bowser, appear. **Jacob** *fights a battle with him . . . and wins!*

I killed the dragon and rescued the *Mario Brothers* Princess on PCP!!! Man!!!!

Triumphant music! **Jacob** *celebrates! The music disappears, and we hear the sound of heartbeats, 180 beats per minute.* **Jacob** *screams.*

My heart felt like it was going to explode, Congregation! Then my grandmother walked up.

We see an image of grandmama.

Grandma, I'm sorry I'm high on PCP!

Congregation, my grandmother, she smiled and said, "You'll be okay, baby, but no more PCP." It was weird 'cause she had been dead for a decade.

Ambulance sounds. Lights. Hospital room. **Dad** *enters.*

Dad Fat man. I came as soon as the word you were hurt hit my ear.

Jacob Seventeen Dad, I can't stop shaking.

Dad PCP makes me shake too. It'll go away soon. Fat man, I have somethin' to tell you. I got this black hole in my chest where my heart used to be. All the horrible things I done are stuffed in it. All the horrible things that's been done to me is stuffed in there too. That black hole, it aches, it hurts. When I do drugs, the pain goes away. For a little while.

Jacob Seventeen Dad, I got that black hole too.

Dad Your grandfather had it. His father had it. I was prayin' God would spare you. When you were born, I held you in this hand, and I looked in your newborn face and saw myself. I told the nurse, "He's gonna be just like me." I was proud. Fat man, I don't want you to be like me. Swear to me, you won't be like me. Swear you won't be like your father. Swear, GODAMMIT!!

Jacob Seventeen I swear!

Dad When you live a life like mine, you attract demons and hellhounds. These hellhounds is chasing me . . .

Dark shadows grow around the theater.

Now I'm afraid they chasing you. I gotta leave here. I'm praying these demons will follow me and leave you be. I'll be back. I'll be back.

Dad *goes to leave.* **Mom** *enters.*

Mom You're alive, Jacob. I'll deal with your PCP-smokin' butt in a minute, but, first, let me pay respects to your father. All hail the king of the addicts. Thanks to you, the hellhounds that are chasing your hell-bound ass are chasing your son too.

Dad Fat man, don't be like me, don't be like ya mother either. Don't be like us. I'll be back. Fat man. I'll be back.

Dad *exits.*

Mom We won't hold our breath. We won't hold our breath!

Jacob Seventeen Mom, can I come home? Just till I feel better?

Mom No. I married a drug addict. There shall be no more drug addicts in my house! We know you not smart. But this is stupid. Is this you trying to be an artist? Is PCP you being an artist? Look what drugs is doing to your father. Look what being an artist did to your father. Jacob, when the world goes to shit, the drug addicts and the artists are the first to be fed to the wolves. The post office is hiring. Here's an application. I'll pray for you, Jacob, but God is not answering my prayers! I don't know what else to do for you. I hope you feel better.

Mom *exits.* **Popeye** *enters.*

Popeye Hey man, how you doin'? You look terrible. I gotta dad joke for you. Might cheer you up. What do you call a line of men waiting for a haircut? A barberque . . .

You don't gotta talk. That's okay. Came to apologize. It's my fault you here. Guy down the block ordered some smoochie poochie laced wit PCP. I sold him the wrong package. So we smoked the PCP. My bad, man.

Beat.

I've been reading a book on reincarnation. You believe in reincarnation? I do. In my next life, Imma be a travel nurse. Imma see the world, heal people. In my next life I wanna fall in love like they fall in love in the movies. Street kid gotta believe in reincarnation.

Pause.

I read *Hamlet* like you asked me to. It was alright. It kinda dragged. But that "To be or not to be" speech, the one you rhymed, I like that. Do I wanna fight to survive, or do I wanna lay down and die an' just be reincarnated? I believe in reincarnation, but I'm afraid to die. To be or not to be, man.

Pause.

They killed Biggie last night. When they killing geniuses, ain't nobody safe. If they'll shoot Biggie, what do you think they'll do to you? What do you think they'll do to me. The crew took a vote . . . you out the crew. Naw, I don't want to hear it. You ain't no street kid. My dad was a street kid. My grandfather was a street kid, and so on, all the way back to the Big Bang. Imma street kid, at least in this life. Jacob, the Black Shakespeare, you out the crew.

Popeye *walks toward* **Jacob**.

Jacob Seventeen Popeye, I need a place to stay.

Popeye My house is your house. You gotta pay some rent, do some dishes. But make sure my house is ya first stop when you get out. Jacob, the Black Shakespeare, I hope you feel better.

Street sounds.

Jacob Narrator Congregation, Popeye's house was my first stop after I got out the hospital. We sat on the porch talkin' 'bout poetry when a man across the street called for Popeye. He wanted some smoochie poochie. When Popeye got across the street, the man pulled out a gun.

We hear a gunshot!

And shot him in the chest. Popeye dropped. We ran to him.

Jacob *falls to the ground.*

Popeye was trying to breathe. He was hurt. Not from bullets. Popeye realized his life was over. He let out a looooong breath.

Jacob *lets out a breath. It echoes throughout the theater.*

Popeye . . . was gone. I watched his blood wind its way through the cracks in the street and drip slowly into the gutter. The crew was a safe space, for a time. 'Cause they were abused like me. Toilet held his hand like this 'cause his dad broke his arm as a little boy. Backwash repeated everything 'cause his mom would abuse him every time he mispronounced a word. Popeye's foster parents locked him in a closet and only opened the door to feed him or beat him. When he was ten years old, they broke his jaw. That's why he talk like dis. We were all drawn to the streets 'cause . . .

. . . you can be what you want to be in the streets, unlike any other place in society. In the streets, I can be a hero, a king, a clown. Shakespeare knew this. Read *Romeo and Juliet*. Shakespeare was an urban poet reporting what he saw. Like Grandmaster Flash, Chuck D. Like Biggie, like Pac. Urban poets reporting what they saw. I'm just an urban poet reporting what I saw. Congregation, my friend Popeye's murder, the PCP, and the pressure of being homeless were getting to me. It cracked my reality. The world looked different, felt different. I was different. I went looking for a safe space.

Lights and music look and sound like they are wound up tight. Music and lights unleash! The vibe of the evening and story have changed. **Jacob** *runs into the light.*

Jacob Casting lady, hi. My name is Jacob. Sorry if I seem scrambled. My friend Popeye was dismantled by bullets three years ago today. Today is the anniversary. For the last three years, I've been struggling to survive. I've run out of options, so, casting lady, it's either Shakespeare or die. So I need to win this audition. Casting lady, what should I be? Should I be me, or should I not be me? In school, the teacher told me that to do Shakespeare, I had to sound like him. I told him that sounded wrong. Maybe that teacher was right. Maybe he was just trying to save my life. 'Cause now I need rent and some food. And Shakespeare is my only way. So, casting lady, if you need me to sound like Ian McKellen and speak the speech with classic classical technique trippingly on the tongue, I'll be Ian McKellen. Watch out, here it comes.

Spotlight hits **Jacob**.

Jacob Classic Hamlet
To be, or not to be: that is the question:
Whether 'tis nobler in the mind to suffer
The slings and arrows of outrageous fortune,
Or to take arms against a sea of troubles
And by opposing end them.

Spotlight goes out.

Jacob Casting lady, if I act in this old-school style, could I gain the globe? What's the price? My soul? It's true, you can feed your soul, but my question is can your soul feed you?

Casting lady, no, wait, don't kick me out. Imma do that speech again, but this time imma pour my dark matter into Shakespeare's canon.

Spotlight hits **Jacob** *again.*

Jacob Urban Hamlet
To be, or not to be, that is the question:
Whether 'tis nobler in the mind to suffer
The slings and arrows of outrageous fortune,
Or to take arms against a sea of troubles
And by opposing end them. To die—to sleep,
To sleep, perchance to dream—ay, there's the rub:
For in that sleep of death what dreams may come.

Spotlight goes out.

Jacob Casting lady, it's Shakespeare or die, and I wanna live, so which version of Hamlet do you prefer? Should I wear Basquiat's crown, and unleash my neo-Black-classical Shakespearian style, even though I hate this caste system? Casting lady, I need a place to sleep! So, if you tell me to, I'll put my soul on ice and be whatever you need me to be: Ian McKellen, Laurence Olivier. Sorry for acting weird, but now I know Tupac and Shakespeare was right: you can die out here. But if Imma die, I wanna die in a play and live to read about it the next day in the *New York Times*. Thank you, casting lady.

Jacob Narrator Congregation, the casting lady loved me. She called me honey.

Casting Director Honey, honey, honey. You're not a Hamlet. Hamlet's a whiny white boy with a little penis. You should play Othello!

Jacob Narrator *Othello* is the one Shakespeare play I was afraid to read. Why? I went to bed upset 'cause I wanted to play Hamlet.

Sounds of morning.

But the next morning, the birds are singing! The sun's beams are beaming! Inspired by nature's artistry, I called up the box office.

Jacob *picks up the phone.*

Yo! I wanna see *Othello*!!! If Othello is my way into the classical world, let's goooo!

The beat drops for the song "You Should Play Othello."

Okay, Congregation, I need your help telling this next part of the story.

"You Should Play Othello" music continues.

So, every time I point at you, you have to say, "You should play Othello. You should play Othello." Let's practice.

Jacob *points at the* **Congregation**.

Congregation You should play Othello. You should play Othello.

Jacob Narrator Great job, Congregation! Okay, here's what happened the night I went to see *Othello*!

The beat kicks up again.

Jacob I put on Jordans and a tie. I'm runnin' to the theater! I buy a ticket—theater's not cheap! I sit in my little uncomfortable seat! POPCORN, PLEASE! The lights go down. My heart starts to pound; this shit's gonna be profound! And a patron in front of me grabs my face and tells me . . .

Jacob *points to the* **Congregation**.

Congregation You should play Othello! You should play Othello!

Jacob The curtain flies out, the lights go up, a white guy walks out. What the fuck? His name's Iago. He must LOVE Othello. Wait! IAGO CAN'T STAND THE NEGRO. He wants to do some real dirty things to Othello. Stop! I bought a ticket to see Othello—why is this dude Iago doing all the talking? OH, shit: Othello married a hot white chick. Her daddy ain't happy! Shakespeare crazy. An usher whispers in my ear lovingly.

Jacob *points to the* **Congregation**.

Congregation You should play Othello! You should play Othello!

Jacob Iago is twisting Othello's mind and turning him against his hot white wife. OH, NO! OTHELLO'S FALLIN' and he can't get up! This Iago's more scary than that clown from the *It* movie. It's intermission. I'm taking a pee, and this guy next to me also draining his willy says to me . . .

Jacob *points to the* **Congregation**.

Congregation You should play Othello. You should play Othello.

Jacob Othello's holding a candle talking about putting out the light. OH, SNAP! He not talking about the candle—he's talking about killing his hot white wife. He's choking her . . . she's dying . . . what's the moral of the story? Interracial marriage is deadly? I coulda stayed at home and watched the OJ documentary for free. The show is over. I'm walking out, and this old lady grabs my butt and shouts . . .

Jacob *points to the* **Congregation**.

Congregation You should play Othello. You should play Othello.

Jacob Outside the theater, I'm full of shock and awe. I just watched Othello choke out his wife and explain it by saying he was "putting out the light." I SHOULD PLAY OTHELLO? What do the Big O and me have in common? OKAY, FULL TRANSPARENCY, I DATE A LOTTA WHITE WOMEN! The audience starts to gather around me. It's a mob now—everyone is jumping up and down, saying . . .

Jacob *points to the* **Congregation**.

Congregation You should play Othello! You should play Othello!

Jacob Stop!!!!!! I run screaming down the block. The audience is chasing me. They're yelling . . .

Jacob *points to the* **Congregation**.

Congregation You should play Othello. You should play Othello.

The echo repeats throughout the theater like a nightmare.

Jacob NOOOOOOOOOOOOOOOOOOOOOO OOOOOOOOO!!!!

"You Should Play Othello" stops. We hear sirens and see police lights.

Police Officer Voiceover THIS IS THE POLICE! PUT YOUR HANDS IN THE AIR!

Jacob Thank God you're here, officer. I'm being chased by Othello fans.

Police Officer Voiceover YOU'RE DISTURBING THE PEACE! PUT YOUR HANDS IN THE AIR.

Jacob Mr. Officer, listen. I went to see *Othello*. It's by Shakespeare. I'm a Shakespearean actor. It's a disturbing play about a white man manipulating a Black man to kill his hot white wife. Everyone in the audience was yelling, "You should play Othello!" That's why I was screaming, "no."

Police Officer Voiceover *Othello*'s a fantastic play. YOU'RE GOING TO JAIL!

Jacob Narrator Congregation, the people from the theater started to gather around, and onlookers began to join the crowd. It was a mob now. The people were cheering. So, I took on the police, 'cause I did nothing wrong!

Police Office Voiceover Mr. Jacob, we googled your IMDb rating. It's very low. SIT DOWN on the ground, OR WE'LL TASE YOU!

Jacob NO! Mr. Officer, I have no weapons except my words, so throw your mistempered weapons to the ground!!! Mr. Officer, the logo on your car says to protect and to serve.

Mr. Officer, if you combine those words, they create the verb "love." But this has more to do with hate than love. Mr. Officer, your misplaced hate has turned to rage. I didn't shoot the sheriff—that was Bob Marley. I didn't sing "911 Is a Joke"—that was Public Enemy. I didn't scream, "Fuck tha Police"—that was Ice Cube. We all look alike, but we isn't a monothetic group. You think we're all monkeys. Come on, dude. Just 'cause monkey see, doesn't mean that monkey do!

Sounds of a cheering crowd. More police lights. A helicopter sound.

Police Office Voiceover Mr. Jacob, this is the Chief of Police. Your use of rhetoric is fucking amazing. But this is your last warning.

Jacob Let me warn you, Chief, like Obi-Wan Kenobi warned Lord Vader, what happens when you strike down a Negro in anger. The good forces launch our souls into the cosmos. There, our souls are transfigured into giant stars and placed in the night sky so we can illuminate the dark streets where people stand alone facing overzealous police. Then for all eternity, we sit on the right-hand side of stars like God, Yoda, and Biggie, as guardians of the galaxy. You may be ON the force, but the force is much stronger with me. So, if you strike me down, I will become more powerful than you could possibly imagine. So, no matter what happens this evening on this street, on Judgment Day, ya gonna have to see me. When I'm sitting on the right-hand side of God! Yoda! And Biggie!

A huge cheer erupts from the crowd.

Crowd JACOB! JACOB! JACOB! JACOB!

Police tase **Jacob**. *Lights flicker.* **Jacob** *is knocked out.*

Jacob Narrator That's what happened the night I went to see *Othello*. The next day I woke up in jail. And I wasn't alone.

We hear the sounds of jail bars closing.

Cellmate Hello, boo, I'm yo cellmate. Excuse my appearance. They don't allow razors in jail. If we met in the streets, you wouldn't recognize me. Imma stunning bitch. You've been sleepin' for hours. I didn't touch you, although I wanted to. Tell me, why was your freedoms filched?

Jacob The police said I was disturbing the peace. People were chasing me, trying to get me to play Othello. It's a play written by Shakespeare. I'm a Shakespearean actor. I fought the police, not with my fists, but my words. To whom shall I complain?

Cellmate To whom? Complain to me honey. Bathe me in your grievances. I beg you! For I am beset, besieged, and beleaguered by boredom. "To whom shall I complain?" *Measure for Measure*, Act Two, Scene Four. I'm an expert on every book the Western world has used to oppress me. The Bible, Shakespeare, *Harry Potter*. I'm a ho. But I'm a well-read ho. Mr. Disturber of the Peace, tell me, is Shakespeare your own personal Jesus?

Jacob He's saved my life. But I don't worship him.

Cellmate Oh, darling, we all get on our knees for something. You kneel at the altar of Shakespeare. Why? Because he wipes away all your sins, your Blackness, your fatness, the stench of the streets that sticks to people like us. With his words, he repaints that adorably ugly face to something . . . adorably mainstream. Tell me, is Shakespeare the white savior of your little Black story?

Jacob He saved my life, and he is white. So, I guess he's my white savior.

Cellmate Oh, Disturber of the Peace, we don't have much time. They'll be releasing you soon, so I must dispatch your Shakespearean-sized delusions with haste. Shakespeare is only the name of an underground writing room, a room filled with fags, queers, Blacks, browns, Jews, and gentiles. Shakespeare was the white paint used to disguise that colorful, rebellious rabble of writers, writing for a small urban city ruled by a wealthy few. So Shakespeare was a queer, nonbinary, multicultural freak! That means he can't be your white savior, 'cause he wasn't all the way white, and in America, if you ain't all the way white, then you all the way Blaaaaaack! I know there was a fierce bitch in that room.

Jacob How do you know that?

Cellmate The words, honey, the words, the words are the proof. Oh! "Come, you spirits that tend on mortal thoughts, unsex me here." "O God, that I were a man! I would eat his heart in the marketplace!" "Let husbands know their wives have sense like them." "When, in disgrace with fortune and men's eyes, I all alone beweep my outcast state, and trouble deaf heaven with my bootless cries, and look upon myself and curse my fate . . . featured like him, like him with friends possessed, desiring this man's art and that man's scope."

Only a soul with a vagina or a soul that wants a vagina could write that. A goddess is caged inside Shakespeare's pale male facade, just like this goddess is caged inside this mannish body. And you, you've wrapped yourself inside an over-bleached Shakespearean fable. 'Cause you, like so many others, need Shakespeare to be white.

Jacob Yeah, I need Shakespeare to be a white. The whiter he is, the more genius he is. The more valuable I am when I speak his words. Shakespeare's just another way of lightening my skin.

Yes, I've been using Shakespeare as a shield. I think that's the only way I've survived. Maybe Shakespeare is a cage, but it's a gilded cage. I feel safer in the cage, is it better to be safe or free?

Cellmate Oh honey, you're not safe or free. You're in jail, with me. Apologies for disturbing your peace, Disturber of the Peace. Don't take it personally. I do this to all my cellmates. I find it's an adequate substitute for sex. But if you care to indulge in an amorous congress with me, in that corner of the cell where we would be unseen . . . no? Okay. Remember, your one call. To whom shall you complain?

Jacob Narrator Congregation, would you rather be safe or free? I had one phone call. To whom shall I complain? I called my dad.

The phone rings. **Jacob** *hangs up. "Taps" plays. A small box of light in the shape of a coffin appears.* **Jacob** *places an American flag over the coffin.*

Jacob Mom? You never told me dad fought in the war. Why are you here?

Mom To pay my respects. Yes, he was a soldier. He was tough, like you. Your father loved Shakespeare, like you. He was an artist, like you. A romantic, like you. He should've been born in the Romantic era, an errant knight, writing poetry, roaming the countryside. Rescuing damsels in distress. But we don't live in a romantic era, Jacob. We live in America, and your father is lying in a cardboard box. If you're not careful, you'll be buried in a cardboard box, too. That is the reality.

Jacob The reality? You kicked me out at sixteen! Reality? My father was shoving drugs into every orifice. Reality? I wouldn't have needed a four-hundred-year-old dead white man if he had been a father, and if you had been a mother!

Mom I was your mother, and I am still your mother. I carried you. I raised you. Shakespeare didn't save you. Look at you! You're unhealthy, you're poor, you have the stench of homelessness! Shakespeare hasn't saved you. You need saving! I'm leaving.

Jacob No, you're gonna listen. You stand there and listen. When Othello killed Desdemona, he said, "I threw away a pearl richer than all my tribe." That line confused me. Now I get it. Othello had no tribe. He was vulnerable. Not safe! That's how Iago fucking got 'em. I keep think you're my tribe. You're not my tribe. Like Othello, I have no tribe.

I'm vulnerable. I'm not safe. Knowing that, mother . . . Valerie . . . a life without you would be better for me.

Pause.

Mom May I have a last word, please? Before you kill me off? My epilogue. What should've been my prologue. For middle school, my father sent me away to boarding school. Every day, I begged him to let me come home. One day, he stopped taking my calls. My heart broke. I was twelve. I never went home again. I've been on my own since. I was nine months pregnant with you, and they rushed me to the hospital. The doctor told me my blood pressure was too high, and if I went forward with the birth both you and I could die. The doctor was willing to try. I said a prayer. God answered with a miracle. We both survived. The nurse placed you in my arms. I looked at you, and Jacob, I felt nothing. I was scared. I thought, "How long do I have to hold this baby?" I was afraid. I didn't want the nurse to see that I felt nothing for my child. I fed you. I clothed you. I changed your diapers. I prayed every day to feel more. I even prayed today. When I met my now ex-husband Clifford, I thought he was my last chance to feel some kinda love. So I threw you out. Jacob, my father never loved me the way I wanted him to, Jacob. And I never loved you the way you wanted me to. And standing here next to you, I still feel nothing. Frailty, thy name is woman. God bless, Jacob. You'll always be in my prayers.

Jacob So I was right. You never loved me.

Music from "The Gun Song" begins.

Jacob Narrator Congregation, remember when I beat that racist acting teacher, how it didn't feel like a victory? It was 'cause I had no tribe, no family, no community to raise my hand in victory!

Congregation, if you have no tribe, where do you get your unconditional love? If you don't have unconditional love, you got nothing. In America, when you have nothing, you supposed to go shopping. I went shopping. I bought a gun.

"The Gun Song." The show goes into concert mode.

Jacob I bought a gun. Why? The gun is how the New World was stole. The Italian said, "This ain't your land. It's my land, bro. Now shut up and show me the gold." When shit hit the fan, the Native man grabbed the arrow an' the bow. Italian said, "That's cute." But the point, red brother, is moot. Let me introduce you to . . . the gun, the gun, the gun.

I bought a gun. Why? The gun is how the West was won. A slave on the run was emancipated by President Lincoln. They gave him a badge 'cause the man was a badass son of a gun. He sent thousands to jail, including his son. In the 1800s, how could the top cop be a Negro, a hero, who died at an old age in his sleep? His name is Bass Reeves. How had this Black man won? You already know. He used: the gun, the gun, the gun.

A gun can kill a Kennedy or a king. It can turn a gorilla into a dictator in an evening. If violence is the universal language of the Western world, the gun is Shakespearean, bro. It can tell your story or end your story. That's why there's a billion guns on the globe. I don't worship this shit, but I live on this planet. That's why I bought a gun.

Doctor's office. Psych ward images.

Jacob What's up, Doc!? I came to you 'cause I'm considering self-slaughter. Just so you know, I'm a Shakespearean actor.

Doctor Mr. Jacob, I'm your doctor. Is that why you bought a gun?

Jacob Yes, Doc. If it were done when 'tis done, Doc, it were well that it were done quickly. If my assassination could trammel up the consequence and catch with my surcease success, that but this blow might be the be-all and the end-all. I don't want to end up a vegetable.

Doctor Why? Why do you want to end it all, Mr. Jacob?

Jacob I don't feel safe, Doc. In school, they taught me Martin Luther King was a man of peace, then they taught me they shot 'em.

Image of Martin Luther King, Jr. shot. Sound of a gunshot.

Malcolm X told us to love ourselves, then they shot him.

Image of Malcolm X shot. Sound of a gunshot.

Medgar Evers? They shot him.

Image of Medgar Evers's bloody driveway. Sound of a gunshot.

Fred Hampton. They shot 'em.

Image of Fred Hampton's bloody mattress. Sound of a gunshot.

If they'll shoot your heroes, they'll definitely shoot you. I'm deathly afraid, Doc. They're flying planes into buildings, Doc. Shakespeare saved me, but he can't save me! Doc, where did my gun go? Suicide seems the like most peaceful way to go.

Doctor Mr. Jacob, I cannot return your firearm. Your family will see to your safety. Mr. Jacob, do you have insurance?

Jacob I need insurance to kill myself? I got no insurance. I don't have enough Equity weeks. I got no family. Doc, I'm ready to die. "Fuck my moms and my girl. My life is played out like a Jheri curl. I'm ready to die." Biggie said that. Then they shot him. "Death is not the greatest loss in life. The greatest loss is what dies inside while still alive." Tupac said that, Doc, then they shot 'em. Self-slaughter seems better than jail or poverty, Doc. But who's gonna pay to bury me? Actors' Equity? I don't want to lay for eternity in an unmarked grave! This self-slaughter thing takes a lot of planning.

Doctor Mr. Jacob, how long have you been feeling this way?

Jacob I was feeling this way yesterday . . . today . . . and I'm sure I'll be feeling this way . . .
Tomorrow, and tomorrow, and tomorrow,
Creeps in this petty pace from day to day,
To the last syllable of recorded time;
And all our yesterdays have lighted fools
The way to dusty death. Out, out, brief candle!
Life's but a walking shadow, a poor player,
That struts and frets his hour upon the stage,
And then is heard no more. It is a tale
Told by an idiot, full of sound and fury
Signifying nothing.

Doctor Mr. Jacob, I have diagnosis. You know your Shakespeare, but do you know your Baldwin?

An image of James Baldwin.

Baldwin said, "It took many years of vomiting up all the filth I'd been taught about myself, and half-believed, before I was able to walk on the earth as though I had a right to be here." You have a right to be here, Mr. Jacob. But know this, your mere presence, your mere presence, is attacking the entire power structure of the Western world. Your spirit is crumbling under the weight of that oppression. That is why you're considering suicide. I'll be committing you to the hospital.

Jacob Narrator Congregation, does anyone feel their presence is attacking the power structure of the entire Western world? Raise your hand. Congregation, that doctor was the first person who told me I had a right to be here. Congregation, play on?

Congregation Play on!

Jacob Narrator I no longer wanted to die. So I broke out of the hospital. It wasn't complicated. I was on the ground floor. I opened the window. There was nurse on a smoke break. So I ran down the Lower East Side.

Jacob *is running as we hear the sounds of cars whizzing by. It's raining.*

I found shelter beneath the Brooklyn Bridge.

Images of under the bridge.

Jacob It felt like all I had left was prayer. But who should I pray to? Can't pray to God. Praying to the creator of the Western world would be odd. To whom shall I complain? Who would listen? Dear Mr. James Baldwin, hear my prayer.

Silence. Then small rumblings.

Although I'm a native son, I'm an invisible man. What are your notes for me? What should I do, Mr. Baldwin? The Western world has been so cruel that death seemed like freedom to me. Because of your words, Mr. Baldwin, I no longer want to die! But what do I do to keep the Western world from slaughtering me? Should I do something so horrible the Western world will think twice before it dares to cause me pain again? Isn't that why human beings seek revenge? Mr. Baldwin, you said revenge is natural. Even nature takes revenge.

Jacob *is interrupted by thunder.*

Mr. Baldwin, rage is rumbling inside. I want to do some notorious type of ill shit. Like Biggie's "Who Shot Ya?"

"Who Shot Ya?" echoes. Pac's "Hit Em Up" echoes. Cube's "No Vaseline" echoes.

Or like the original diss track, Aaron the Moor. Hurting a man might be my thing. Vengeance is pounding in my chest. Retribution in my head. Here, at the witching hour underneath the Brooklyn Bridge, against the entire Western world, I declare: I need, I want, I must have revenge!!!

Thunder. **Jacob** *falls to his belly.*

Is that you, God, warning me?

Silence.

Or is it you, Mr. Baldwin, affirming me?

Rumbling thunder. **Jacob** *stands.*

Mr. Baldwin, from the cosmos, please speak plainly. Should I seek revenge against the Western world!?

EXTENDED LOUD THUNDER! **Jacob** *celebrates!*

Yes, Mr. Baldwin, revenge. Crack your cheeks! Spout 'til you have drenched our steeples.

Thunder crack.

HELP ME! Strike flat the thick rotundity o' the world!

Thunder crack.

Crack nature's molds. Rumble thy bellyful!

Thunder crack.

RUMBLE!! RUMBLE!!! Mr. Baldwin, spit fire! Spout rain!

Thunder crack.

Let the lights go down on Broadway. Let Hollywood burn. Through cruelty will I seek out my fame! Mr. Baldwin, that's all that's left for a poor player who has already strutted and fretted his hour upon the stage! I'll be a public enemy and fight the powers that be. Revenge, Mr. Baldwin, until I bring the Western world to its knees! Revenge! As I live and breathe, I want revenge!! Revenge!! Revenge!!!!!!

Storms! Rain!

Jacob Narrator Congregation, before I turned completely to the dark side, I went back to church. I called God.

Jacob *returns to church. A light shines on a red phone.* **Jacob** *walks to the phone and dials. The pew is visible.*

Jacob God, I'm not praying to you. This is a negotiation. This black hole in my chest is killing me. I don't have much time. I need a quick resolution. Here are my terms. I demand justice, not just for me, but for all righteous beings on the globe. If you don't meet my terms, like Shylock, I must confess, I will take a pound of flesh! It is dearly bought. I can't turn the other cheek, God. I want reciprocity, God. Justice, God. Answer me, God! Shall I have it!? Call me back!

Jacob Narrator I went to wait for God's answer. That's when the black hole struck. It was killing me, like it had killed my father and all my grandfathers.

We hear and see the sound of the black hole. **Jacob** *falls to the ground.*

I close my eyes. I'm dying, but I'm cool with it.

The church rumbles. The light flickers. Weird images appear. A light on **Jacob**.

Dad Booming Voiceover Fat man! Open your eyes.
I am thy father's spirit,
Doomed for a certain term to walk the night,
And for the day confined to fast in fires,
Till the foul crimes done in my days of nature
Are burned and purged away.
I could a tale unfold whose lightest word
Would harrow up thy soul, freeze thy young blood,
Make thy two eyes, like stars, start from their spheres.

Jacob You're here to help me take my revenge.

Dad Booming Voiceover NO!

Jacob I hate you!

Dad Booming Voiceover Get that hate out ya heart!!! It's killing you!!!

The floor rumbles. The room shakes. **Jacob** *falls to the ground.*

Jacob I don't have a heart. I got a black hole where my heart used to be!

Dad Booming Voiceover That black hole is what I willed you. That's why I begged the angels to let me come to you! To help save your life. Look upon these waters!

Sounds of waves crashing.

Your ancestors are waiting for you. They've always been with you. Your hurt, your hate, your rage blinded you to their existence.

Dad *disappears.*

Jacob Narrator Congregation, my dad's spirit brought me to the edge of a sea. My grandmother was standing on the water summoning me.

Projected image of the grandmother.

Congregation, I walked on the water toward her, and behind my grandmother I saw thousands of ancestors, a tribe. Not just my aunts and uncles but Basquiat, Baldwin, Biggie, and one white dude, William Shakespeare. My grandmother was gathering them all unto me. My tribe wrapped their arms around me. My grandmother put her hands in the sea and poured the sea over me. Cleansing me. The black hole in my chest was gone. My tribe gave me a new heart. Then, Congregation, some dope music hit, and me and my tribe danced on the waters. Congregation, I finally found unconditional love.

Jacob *dances and celebrates with his ancestors. He is saved!*

Dad Booming Voiceover Fat man, remember me, remember me! Fat man. I told you I'd come back. Remember me!

His words echo throughout the theater.

Jacob Remember thee?
Ay, thou poor ghost, whiles memory holds a seat
In this distracted globe. Remember thee!
Yea, from the table of my memory
I'll wipe away all trivial fond records,

All saws of books, all forms, all pressures past.
That youth and observation copied there,
And thy commandment all alone shall live
Within the book and volume of my brain,
Unmixed with baser matter. Yes, by heaven!
Remember thee. Yes, by heaven.

Jacob *lies down on the pew and closes his eyes. There's knocking on the church door.* **Jacob** *sits up. He is back in reality.*

Jacob Narrator Someone's knocking, Congregation. Play on.

Congregation Play on!

Jacob *opens the door. An* **Old Woman** *using a walker and her* **Grandson** *walk in.*

Old Woman Hallelujah, hallelujah. Me and my grandson was outside. My feet is tired. My back aching. We was knockin' on the door. The Devil, that sneaky motherfucka, had locked the door. Then you came like an avenging angel an open that door. Hallelujah! First miracle of the day. Won't be the last.

The **Old Woman** *and the* **Grandson** *walk to the pew.*

Oooooooo. Feels good to sit. Sit wit' me, grandson.

The **Old Woman** *and the* **Grandson** *sit.*

You need to sit too. That's a big, beautiful belly hangin' off you. I know your feet hurt.

All three characters sit on the church pew.

We loooove you. Don't we, grandson?

Grandson We love you, man.

Jacob You don't even know me.

Old Woman Ooo! We don't need to know you to love you. What's your name? You know what, don't you tell me! We love you, whatever your name is. Without reservation, conditions, and none of that annoying fine print at the bottom of my phone bill. We love you! Tell 'em, grandson.

Grandson We love you, man!

Jacob I guess I love you too.

Old Woman Ooooo! You guess? You guess? When you tell someone you love 'em . . . you say it with conviction. With all ya heart an' soul. You don't say, "I guess." Tell me you love me again!

Jacob I love you!

Old Woman And we love you! Whatever yo name is. Tell 'em, grandson.

Grandson We love you, man.

The **Old Woman** *stands, grabs her walker, and begins to walk into the chapel.*

Old Woman 'Cause the door was locked! And now it's open. Thank you, Jesus, for sending whatever his name is! Hallelujah, hallelujah, hallelujah.

The **Grandson** *follows the* **Old Woman** *into the side chapel, then comes back out.*

Grandson She's gonna be in there a while. She got hundreds of people to pray for. Then she'll sing for hours. You like music!? I make beats! I'm sellin' CDs—five dollars each. Name's Lincoln. I'm sellin' them 'cause my grandmama's got . . . cancer. I gotta get her the better insurance. These beats is the only way I got. I used to get in trouble a lot. My mom kicked me out. Grandma said, "You don't throw away babies!" Grandma packed my bags. We took one bus, two subways, walked three miles to where grandma stay. She said, "Drop your bags, look me in the eye! I love you, Lincoln." She screamed it. "I love you, Lincoln! No matter what you do, what you say, where you go, I'll love you. And when I die, my love will only grow. My love is infinite, eternal." That night, in bed, I decided I'd become President of the United States. President Lincoln the Second, the first Black president! Imma save my grandma, then Imma save the world! It all starts with sellin' these beats. Five dollars each. What do you do?

Jacob Imma Shakespearean actor. What happened with your mother?

Grandson You know your hip-hop history? Tupac an' Biggie was boys. They had beef. If they hugged it out, the world be different. Me an' my mom hugged it out. Now the world is different. It's only like zero-point one percent different. But it different.

Jacob Lincoln, I'll be back, and I'll buy some CDs.

Jacob *runs as if he has somewhere important to be. He stops. He raises his hand as he's about to knock on a door. The door suddenly opens.*

Hi. Shakespeare usually ends his comedies with an act of forgiveness, and my life has been a comedy of errors. I've been walking around thinking nobody's ever been hurt like me. But you've been hurt, your father hurt you, his dad hurt him, and so on and so forth, all the way back to the Big Bang. Someone has to be brave enough to be the last person to be hurt. I thought the Western world and God decided who plays the hero and who plays the villain. We decide.

Valerie, Mom, if I could forgive you, and you could forgive me, we could change the world by zero-point one percent.

Lights come up, **Jacob** *walks toward the* **Congregation**. *Music. The music continues to swell during this final section.*

Jacob Narrator Congregation, I could tell you what happened next. But it doesn't matter what happened next. Some people ask me, "How could you forgive your mother?" My answer? What would happen to me if I didn't forgive my mother? Shakespeare saved my life. It's true. The moment I forgave my mother and freed myself from all the anger and rage saved my life and gave me the strength to . . .

Jacob *points to the* **Congregation**.

Congregation Play on!

Jacob Narrator Performing this play every night reminds me of all the people who saved my life. The teacher who made me read that Henry the Fifth speech. The doctor who told me I have a right to be here! Popeye! They're the reason I'm able to stand in front of you today. They saved my life and gave me the strength to . . .

Jacob *points to the* **Congregation**.

Congregation Play on!

Jacob Narrator I'm grateful for the boy who taught me that one act of forgiveness could change the world by zero-point one percent. That boy is why I'm able to stand in front of you today. He saved my life, and he gave me the strength to . . .

Jacob *points to the* **Congregation**.

Congregation Play on!

Jacob Narrator This play is my way of paying all that back. I believe this story can save a life and give someone the strength to . . .

Jacob points to the **Congregation**.

Congregation Play on!

Inspirational music swells.

END OF PLAY

Jacob Ming-Trent in Conversation with James Shapiro and Kathryn Vomero Santos

James Shapiro (JS): Could you tell us about the early meetings you had while you were developing this play? What kinds of feedback were you getting?

Jacob Ming-Trent (JMT): At first, people really didn't understand what I was trying to create and, to be honest, I don't think I understood what I was trying to create. I wanted to tell my story, but I knew I wanted to tell it for a purpose. I thought there was another kid out there who needed to hear it, a young actor who needed to hear it, a young hip-hop artist, a young painter, a young whoever who needed to hear it and that my story could save their life. That's why I called it *How Shakespeare Saved My Life*.

Early on, I had ideas about using projections, weaving in tons of music, and folding Shakespeare into my story in a way that people hadn't heard before. At one point or another, I was told to cut it all—the projections, the music, the Shakespeare. They just wanted to see me dressed in all black on stage with a chair. But that was not what I wanted. I wanted a fresh, modern, updated idea of theater with audience participation. When you're writing stuff like this, people are gonna have tons of opinions, because they're all bringing money to the table, but, as a creator, you really have to stick to your guns and at least explore what you originally wanted to do. And then if it needs to change, you can change it. But I'm glad I stuck to my guns, because my instincts were right.

Kathryn Vomero Santos (KVS): When I first met you, you had just played Falstaff to great acclaim in the Public Theater's 2021 production of *Merry Wives*, and you shared that you wanted to write a memoir about your journey with Shakespeare. But that initial idea to write a memoir has morphed into this play. What led you from memoir to play?

JMT: The memoir idea felt daunting. I was only around forty or forty-one when that thought first surfaced, and I knew I still had more of my journey ahead. I didn't set out deliberately to write a play or a one-person show either. I was in the Berkshires working on some other writing, and friends came up to visit. They asked me to tell stories from my childhood, stories I hadn't really told anyone. So, I started to write. Because I write television and film scripts and I work in theater, the script form made sense as a way to tell my story. It allowed me to inhabit the story as performer and writer simultaneously, and that combination felt right. The theatrical form also lets the story breathe in a communal space, which is important to the themes I'm exploring. The first sixteen pages or so came out quickly. I sent them to two theater companies on a whim, and to my surprise, both commissioned the work immediately. That put me on the hook. Brave people got into the foxhole with me and pushed the project forward.

JS: So is this play straight autobiography?

JMT: Most of it is. The story takes place over the span of about ten years or so, but what that means is that I had to fit all that lived time into 90 minutes. So, some things had to be massaged and moved around, but most of it, probably 90 percent, is true. We delve into things, but we can't tell the whole stories of those events, so we have to find theatrical ways of moving through them, tying one event to another event. There may have been two years between those points, but in this show, they happen rapidly within five minutes. So yeah, it's my life told in a very hyper-theatrical way. The thing I tell people is that things were far worse than what I put in the play. This is the PG-13 version but still mostly true.

KVS: Tell us about your process. How did the play develop? What happened to the script when you started workshopping and performing it?

JMT: It was about two continuous years of writing supplemented by workshops and revisions. For me, writing is more than putting words on a page. It's meditation. It's walking around with a voice recorder and notes in your phone. It's persistent reflection and a lot of conversations with smart people from many walks of life. I intentionally built a community around this work. It took a village: dramaturgs, directors, musicians, actors, designers, friends, scholars, and mentors across the country. When I picked up the phone, people answered, and that collaborative support shaped the play.

When we moved into rehearsal and performance, the script continued to change. I rewrote perhaps half of it while on my feet. Having been an actor for thirty years, I'm very aware of how language manifests in the body. Some lines felt right on the page but didn't land live. Some scenes needed to be removed or restructured. The piece shifted from a literary document to a performance document. It needed to function when I was moving through space, interacting with props, music, and the audience. That process was both exhilarating and humbling. Even now it feels alive. As I grow, the piece grows, and I continue learning why my soul needed to write this.

JS: What about the piece changed over the course of these many drafts?

JMT: Initially we imagined the show as a kind of Gil Scott-Heron-style piece: me with a live band, blending song, rap, poetry—a performance-art tableau that felt like a 1960s or 1970s happening. That version evolved through many permutations: there was a band, then a DJ, then no music ensemble at all. Over time we realized that the ideas I was expressing were complex and the audience needed clearer access to the narrative arc. So the piece moved toward a more traditional, Brechtian theatrical structure. It's still rhythmic and musical, but it now uses some conventional theatrical devices to guide the audience through difficult emotional and social terrain. The result is a hybrid piece: it's musical and poetic, yet dramaturgically intentional.

KVS: Who are your models? Who influenced you as an artist, and whose influences can we see in this play?

JMT: Shakespeare is obviously central. Brecht is a major influence for the structural idea of making an audience think rather than simply feel. Hip-hop artists from a certain era like Public Enemy, Mos Def, Tupac, and Biggie influenced me not necessarily for their songs but for their worldview as urban poets. Their work holds a mirror up to society and insists on humanization. It's political, personal, and poetic. That tradition goes back to blues artists like Robert Johnson and Son House, who told stories about survival, making impossible choices, and the costs of fame and survival. My character Jacob uses these artists as a kind of lifeline when he feels that he might have to sell his soul in order to make it.

Visual artists like Jean-Michel Basquiat and musical giants like Ella Fitzgerald also influence how I assemble language. Basquiat constantly quoted and recontextualized other images. Fitzgerald could quote dozens of songs within a single performance. I borrow that technique, quoting, juxtaposing, and reusing lines to place them into new contexts. The play becomes a web of references that creates a historical and emotional frame for my story.

JS: Can you tell us more about the title, *How Shakespeare Saved My Life*?

JMT: When I began writing the title felt literal: Shakespeare did save my life. But as I investigated, I discovered the saving forces were broader than one writer. The play begins with Shakespeare as an active lifeline and then expands outward to include many people and traditions that sustained me. Part of the project is to demystify Shakespeare and the power he holds within our society. Because we perceive him to be this genius white man, one's ability to master his words, to unlock his genius with your own intellect, becomes a sign of worthiness. I believe that actually anybody can speak his words, so my play is a kind of unmasking of Shakespeare and all that he signifies. It's bringing Shakespeare off the pedestal and adding other people to the canon that I feel are just as important to their generation as Shakespeare was to his. We do all sorts of things with Shakespeare in this play. We break Shakespeare. We do it traditionally. We flip it upside down. We set it to music. I use the lines in other contexts, so the lines have other meanings. I love Shakespeare, but I am not bowing to him in the play. And in that way, it's actually kind of invigorating, because it unlocks him for so many people.

KVS: We're going to church, but we're not worshipping Shakespeare.

JMT: Yo, that's exactly right. Yes.

KVS: What do you hope audiences and readers will take away from your play? What do you hope that they'll be motivated to do after they see or read it?

JMT: The piece is ultimately an invitation: come with your preconceived notions, let them be disrupted, and allow a blend of Shakespeare, hip-hop, and personal story to open a new way of seeing and hearing. I hope people leave inspired to tell their own stories—to write, paint, rap, or otherwise create. I want the audience to sit with questions about forgiveness, about the people who have saved their lives, and about how they might be a lifeline for others. For me this play is an act of giving back. It's my way of paying forward what was given to me. I want to see audiences challenge what feels unchallengeable: hierarchies in the arts, cultural myths about who belongs in the canon, the idea that certain forms are only for certain people. If the play prompts even one person to open a notebook, join a class, or reach out to an artist they admire, it has done its work.

March 2026

www.ingramcontent.com/pod-product-compliance
Ingram Content Group UK Ltd.
Pitfield, Milton Keynes, MK11 3LW, UK
UKHW062031110826
474319UK00001B/1

9 781350 595941